Confluence

by Edith H. Lamprecht

Illustrated by Karen S. Marshall

Confluence

The dictionary defines "Confluence" as "the meeting or junction of two streams", as when two streams come together to form a river.

Similarly, these writings describe the merging of our Life Experiences throughout our Lifetime, from Birth's Innocence ("The Little One's Eyes"), to Life's Struggle ("Emergence"), to Transformation ("Centurion's Volcano"), and the Impact of Loving Another ("Finding My Love"), and of Universal Love ("We Are One"). Some of these poems grapple with Life's Biggest Questions including "The Right to Life".
It is Our Hope that, ultimately, these poems, will Lift You Up and Leave You Full of Light, Love, and Forgiveness.

As you travel through these profound writings and illustrations, you, too, will experience the diverse journey of life they depict and you, too, will feel the mergence and meaning of it All, at Life's End. The Common Thread throughout "Confluence" is the Convergence of the Human and the Divine.

Dedication

This book is dedicated to the Cosmos - the Earth, Sun, Oceans, Moon, Stars, and Galaxies, and Great Spirit, who Give us Life and Creative Inspiration.
May it Open a Portal to the Universal Love Shared By Us All.

Spanning a Lifetime, these Writings are meant for All Those Who Have Come Before, All Those Who Are With Us Now, and All Those Who Will Be With Us in the Future.

A Special Thanks to our Family and Friends whose encouragement gave us the endurance to make "Confluence" a Reality.

"Confluence" is a collection of poignant free verse poems traversing our quintessential Universal Journey from Birth to Death - and Beyond.

These poems give inspiration to the "Ordinary", as well as addressing social issues affecting All of Us.

Embracing our human struggles and bringing Light to our Humanity and our Divinity, these poems speak to the Universal Love that holds us all together.

"Confluence" leads us to a place of Transcendence and Inner Peace.

Praise for Confluence

Edie Lamprecht takes us on a journey of leaping, flying, dancing, growing, grieving, forgiving, believing, celebrating, affirming to make meaning of our lives. Confluence is a collection of poems with Living as its theme and Hope its message. I love her analogy of two rivers coming together, to represent our life experiences, past and present, converging into something strong and whole. Nature is my happy place and Edie's poems take me there where the divine can be accessed by us humans. Her beautiful free flowing poetry, together with the elegant illustrations, makes this collection one to be cherished.

Margaret Cooney PhD

Edith Lamprecht's profound spiritual connection with the Universe touches one deeply. It's reflective of nature's message to open our hearts and feel the Spirit Message of Oneness. It leaves the reader wanting more, as we witness her journey to be our own...after all...we are "ONE."

The artist's tender embrace of the text is most impressive. This is a keeper to be read again and again.

Rev. Norma Connolly

Edith Lamprecht's writings are a record of her life journey. She marks the "confluences," the points in time, the experiences on her path, with words and images. Her "confluences" speak to all of us bringing remembrances of first love, later loves, marriage, birth, Dad's high boots, a Mother's autumn soul lesson, family, life, death, transformation, renewal. Edith's voice speaks with deep feeling wrapped in images of Mother Nature and the elements. Spirit's connective thread, exuding tenderness and love, weaves meaning between the words and images bringing the journey's story gently home in all of us. "Confluence" is a book to put by your bedside to welcome the morning rise or the evening darkness with a centering reflection.

Jacqueline L. James, MA

Index

Leaping

Let Me Tread Lightly
 Over the Earth-
Dancing through
 The Dark Times
Leaping Across
 The Abyss
 Of Betrayal / Deception
 Not Ignoring
 But
 Not Embracing-
My Footprints Will Not Be There.

Holding Lightness in My Heart
My Feet will Imprint the Ocean's Sand-
Where the Wind Tastes My Dreams,
The Tides Exalt Life's Mystery
And the Ocean's Salt
 Quenches My Appetite
 For Life and Love.

Leave My Footprints
On The Shores
 Of Possibility
Where My Visions
 Are My Truth.

The Light

The Fire of Life

In the Beginning
We Birth
The Fire Of Life
Some need the care of others to tend their fire
And to Keep it Alive.
Others burst into flames full-force.

Over Time -
We Struggle to Keep our Breath - Winds
Strong, Our Ego Fire
Competing to Be
The Biggest & Best.
Sometimes Even taking the Wood / Life Force
From Others
To Be the Most Brilliant.

Will we remember that Our Power lies not in the Big Flame
But in the Divine Sparks?

Sometimes we Believe
Our Mighty Fire Is Immortal
That We Can Beat
The Others
And Burn-on Forever.

Toward the End
When Our Fire Subsides
When the Ego Dimmers
And the Soul Life Emerges
As the Embers Glow
Reflecting the Stars
In the Evening Sky...
It is Now that the Fire is
Most Powerful.

Most do not Know,
Do not Realize
This Power
That Lies
In the Ending.

3

Circle of Life

At Dawn,
    You were born with balding head
        and Knowing Eyes
    You came so Peacefully
        to us

    Only the doctors brought your cries.

As you Grow,
    We Teach each other.

    You show me the Truth
        of the Moment.

    I try to provide consistency

    For the Open Expression
        of Your Personality.

During those adolescent
    years of turbulence,

    You develop Your Own Social Conscience

    Once again, you pull me
        back and forth,
    At once distant, and then close.

Becoming An Adult,
    Your own children to be

    You now see my Real Humanity

    And, for the first time,
    I see Your Eyes in Me.

May you Create
    Your Own Vision
    To pass on to them

And to carry you through
    the Midday Sun.

As You Grow Older,
    Once Again
    Returning
    to your newborn baldness
     and
    Eyes of Light

This time, with
    New Wisdom

As You Pass Into the Night.

Out of Hope

Out of Hope, we are Born
That our struggles will be easier
Than those of our parents;
That we may affirm the Strengths
Of their Existence.

And soon we must discover
        The Myths of Our Upbringing;
That Home is no longer Our Origin
That Home is not "Outside"...
That Home is only Inside Ourselves--

And in the few we touch
        Those moments are rare
When minds meet, and bodies--
We Seek Our Reality to Share.

And in those Minutes
Of Affirmation
We Say "Yes" to Life.

Amidst our illusions and confusions
We struggle to Become
We fight Time's Battle
Regrets of the Past
Fears of the Future
Searching to Find
Our Reason for Being.

In Our Confirmation
Our Life has a Meaning
We then Give Birth
To Another, with Hope
That his Load
Will Be Lighter.

The Little One's Eyes

This I have learned from the Little One's Eyes;
We all hold Our Truth Inside.

The Challenge is to Trust
The Song Inside
And Let it "Sing-Out"--
Even Against the Tide.

For the Growing Emerges
It's Own Way
Not from Making
A Structure
To Stay.

What Can I Give
If this Be the Case?
A Reflection,
An Affirmation
Of Each Inner Self.

Not Answers, but Questions
And Faith that We All
Hold Our Very Own Truth
Inside Ourselves.

Dad's High Boots

I Need Your High Rubber Boots Dad
Those Tall Black Ones that Stood
In the Farmhouse Woodshed
The Ones You Slipped into at Sunrise
On those Rainy Muddy Days
The Ones Just Meant
For Mucking the Horse Stalls
And Trudging
Through the Garden
At Dawn.

May I Borrow Your
High Boots Dad
To Get Through
My Murky Muddy
Life?

The Adirondack Yen

Radiant Warm Soft Summer Air
Soothing
Our Midday Walk

Comforting Pine-Tree Scents
Inviting Us Into
A Nestling Nap
Of Memories

Of Magical Paths
In Corey's Forests.

Dad's Corncob Pipe
Blending Into
The Trees, The Lake
The Days.

The Ancient Blue Rock
The Site
Of Fish Decimation
Promising
Our Sumptuous
Morning Breakfast.

Campfires Fragrance
At Day's End
Snuggling into Sleeping Bags

Anticipating
An Everlasting
Tomorrow.

Prairie Sunrise

Heart Fire
    Emerging
    Embracing
    the Morning
Red Edges
    Breaking
    Across
    Mountains
Blue Sky
    Side-By-Side.

The Life Sounds
    of
    My Breathing
    Penetrating
    the Dawn.

Each Breath
    Expanding
    For Miles
    Tapping
    the Well-Spring
    Of Life.

The Intense, Steady
    Heartbeat
    of the Earth's
    Core
Providing
    Forbearance
    This Day

Landscape's Consistency
    Giving
    Peace, Comfort.

At the Pond

Like the Smallest Pebble
   On a Windward Beach
What can my Impact be-
   Beyond a pebble's reach?

But my Soul is an Ocean
   Expansive, Vast, and Deep.

My Spirit is an Open Door;
   and in my Dreams I Fly.

So, to the World I can give
My LOVE is Infinite.

We Are One

I came to the Beach Today
Me and Hundreds of Others
Basking in Summer's Essence
Soaking - Up the Universal Sun

Bursting with the Sounds
Of Latino, Africano / Americano
Music Mingling with
Children's Squeals
At the First Tastes of the
Summer Sea
And melding with Girlfriend's Giggles
Knee - Deep in Waves.

The Smells of Salami, Collard Greens, Pasta and
Beer
Wafting Deliciously into the Salty Sea Air.

An Eagle's View of Smells, Colors, Songs
And Flavors
All Blending Together
Under the Magnetic Sun

With the Wind Quietly Whispering
"We Are One."

A Celebration of Vows

Families Gathering Together
  From Life's Far Corners
To Witness their Ceremony
  A Wedding of Lives
The Golden - locks Bride
  And Athletic Groom
Brought Us Here
  To this Midwest City
Centering Us Again
  To What Really Matters.

Their Lives Merged
  And Ours Converged
Our Energies Poured
  Into Their Rings
A Promise of Fulfillment.

Their Vows Stated
  Reinstating Ours.
And With Them
  We Pronounce
"I Do."

We Do
Promise to
Stand By these Two
And To Hold Each Other
Lovers, Friends, Spouses
  And Family
In Our Energetic Love
Forever.

The Everlasting Christmas Tree

On Christmas Eve Day we planted the tree;
Its branches mere buds we could barely see.
"It's too late" they all said; for tomorrow is Christmas Day.

When its roots touched the ground
The Nourishment Began.
With Mother Earth's Soil,
And Cosmos Sun and Rain
All fed by Our Longing for a Better Way.

And the Tree Begged for More,
To keep Growing to the Sky
By Christmas Morning.

Spreading the Word,
The Wind Blew Hope
Around the World.
Suddenly The Tree's Lights Appeared
Their glowing colors emerging
As people began shedding
Their sadness and despair.

On Christmas Morning
The Branches
Were Reaching the Sky
Embracing Us All
With Truth's Words
Singing-Out:
May Peace and Love
Reign Forevermore.

Estero Inspiration

At first glance the Seascape Unshackles Life's Grip
Sounds of Lapping Waves Awakening Us at Sunrise
Urging Endless Beach Walks with sand between our toes
Dolphins and Pelicans Enlivening Our Trip.

The Language of the Winds and palm trees
Merge with the Laughter of Camaraderie
Unloosening Earthly Ties
And Opening the Soul to Freedom.

No Boundaries on the Horizon
Only Possibilities
And the Sunset Kisses Us Good Night.

Emergence

The Ocean Waves
In their Angry Surge
Reflect the Turbulence
Inside My Soul

They throw my body
Against the Shore
To return it again,
Contorted
Upon Myself
Back out to Sea.

Folded - in
The Ocean's Wave,
My Body Recoils
Back into the womb
Of water
Surrounding it.

With Each Surge
Is thrown
My Inner Rage
Only to be thrown
Again with
Newfound Pain.

Each time I Return
With Greater Separation
Back to my Beginning.

How long must I endure
This pounding intrusion
Upon My Soul ???

Until this rhythm of
Anger, sadness, healing
Completes Itself
And I Emerge
Cleansed with
Newfound Hope
In a Rebirth of My Soul.

War's Children

O Little Children
        Both Young and Old
Your Grief is our Own.

In Your Eyes
        I See
        The World's Sadness
the Needy, the Hunger, the Homeless.

Your Tears call Forth Our Compassion.

Your Wounds Tearing, Searing,
        Our Soul's Injury.

You are Begging Us to Open
        Our Eyes and See
Our Inner Child Cries Out for Peace.
It is the Answer for the Universe.

War

Knees Shaking
Hearts Pounding
Insides Quaking

War is an Outrage
Of Raging Within
This Continent

What about The Children?
Their Pain is Our Own.
When Will We Learn
Our Protection and Care
Is Their Future.

There is a Deep Sadness
A Grieving Deep - Down
Within Every Person
In the World Right Now.

What Right Have a Few
To Endanger So Many ?

When we Focus On Peace
We Won't Need War
Anymore.

Amen

Woundings

The Big Boogie-Man
Haunts Us All

Deep Inside Us
the Goop of First Woundings

Have Morphed And
Disformed
Into

A Monster
We keep
Hidden

In a Pen
Of Deep Hurts,

With Certain Times and Triggers
The Goop Leaks Out
Even a Glimpse
Freaking-Out
Passers-By.
Seeping-Out
and Contaminating Our Lives.

If Only We Could
Let it ALL Out

We'd See that
Others Carry Monsters too

And Sharing Them
Would
Make Us Free
They Are Our Affinity.

Unraveling

Yet another teenager shooting ripping through the News
As the World Turns again from its Reflection.
Our Image is in Each of these Tragedies.
How Many Cries for Help
Before We Disassemble Our Own Madness?
Each Killing Spree Pulls at the Fabric of Society
Unraveling the Falsehoods of "Success";
Our Status - Hungry Society
Creating Our Blindness
And Emptying Our Hearts
Of What Really Matters
Of the Truth of Our Being
When Will We Turn from the Goal of Sameness
To the Celebration of Differences?

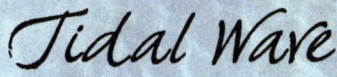

Tidal Wave

It starts with Ripples
Of Uncertainty
Slight Changes in the
Ocean Currents
Then -- A Riptide or Two
Takes you Under
Your head in Your Hands
For Protection.
And We Stand-By
Beginning to take Notice
Of Your Gurgles.

Watching you Struggle
To regain
Your Life-Breath;
Some Fearfully Run Away
Others Stand-By
Exclaiming "Oh My !"

A Few of Us Warriors
Charge into the Water
Our Bodies
Desperately Grabbing
At Your Thrashing Body...
Trying to Pull You to Safety.

But you have Surrendered
Your Body is Limp
And It is Too Late...
The Tidal Wave Arrives
Pounding to Shore
Pulling You Under
And Throwing
Your Mind Into Chaos...
Succumbing to Psychosis.

Soul Survival

How Will You Steal my Soul

Will you Kidnap Me
And take Me away-

Separating Me from My Own
So I Won't Contaminate
Your World?

Will You fill Me With
Chemicals trying
to Suffocate My Soul?

Will You Shock Me, Mock Me,
Jolt Me
to Reframe My Brain?

My Soul Will Survive
My Soul Will Arise
Again & Again

Your Soul Fears Mine
Yet We Are the Same.
Your Soul Sees
It's Reflections In Me

It Is Your Fears
that Feed Your Methods-
A Travesty Gone Wrong
And the Tragedies go On & On.

Can't You See
You Cannot Win
In the End
Your Efforts Are
to No Avail

Because My Soul is Eternal.

Choosing the Miracle

Hearing the "Experts"

Listening to My Self.

Is this Experience Frustrating

Or Enlightening?

Going Beyond What's Heard

And Listening

To What's Known.

I Choose to Believe

That the Healing has Begun.

This Miracle

Both Time and Space

Transcends

May Baffle the Experts.

It's in God's Hands

Where we are Safe,

And Truth we Know

Of Perfect Love,

Healing the Soul.

Amen

An Oak Tree Felled

An Oak Tree Felled...

Its' Multi-generational Roots Torn from the Bowels of the Earth
      With Tentacles Entwined, Enmeshed...
It Took a Major Storm of Hurricane Proportions
      To Reveal the Misperceptions.
Of Centuries-old Control -Covered Misconceptions.

With Roots Unveiled...
      It's Nourishment Stifled...
          The Umbilical Cord Broke...
             Suffocating the Tree of Unspoken Myths.

All that is left is the Bloodied Forest Bottom...
      The War Zone of the Storm...
          Allowing Death to What Was...

Surrendering to the Mystery...
      Slowly, Tentatively, & with Unmeasured Courage
          New Plantings Form
             On the Forest Floor...

Created by Incessant Struggle...
      And Fed by Surrender and Trust...
          And Awareness to Avoid the Bloodied Ground.

The Pine Trees are Slowly Emerging...
      Lifted-Up By Her Sister Trees
          Divinely Designed to Catch those Giving-up/Throwing-Up
          Their Souls to God.

Held-up to the Heavens for Transformation, Renewal, New Life.

And So It Is.

Amen.

Centurion's Volcano

Who put the Spin
On the Mind's Forehead
A Seductive Subconscious
Imprint;
Society's Paradigm
Sanctioning Follower's
Frozen Minds
To Blithely Meld
Without Forethought?

Suffering a Poison
Punished with Banishment
No Struggle Condoned
No Meaning Remaining.

Until the Few Dissidents
Create a Crack
The Fumes of Staleness
Start Seeping -Out
The Roles and Stereotypes
Revealing Odorous Distortions.

The Crack Now Pressurized
With Incremental Numbers
Sickened by the Status Quo.

The Many Now Seeing
With Hearts
The Lies, The Wars
The Comfort Zone
Manifested.

The Fracture
Becoming a Fissure
Emptying Minds
Birthing
A Vision
That Only
The Heart
Can Hold.

The Right to Life

Who has the Right
  to take a Life?

Can I take Yours
  or take my Own?

Can you take mine?

No Matter What
  The Soul Survives,
  The Body dies.

Suicide or Murder?
  Both leave Behind
  a Wake of Woundedness.

Those Left Behind
  Must Pay the Price
  Of An Unfinished Life.

Those Departed Souls
  Must Transform
  And Return to Try Again.

Purging Life's Sorrows

If I could Pull You Forth
   From the Heavens
I'd Look Into Your Eyes
I'd Tell You - Now I Know
   Of Your First Woundings
   Stealing Your Passions
   And Leaving Your Young Heart
   Barricaded and Broken.

         Together, We Would Weep
         And, Entwining Our Hands
         Over Your Heart's Gushing Wounds
         Our Tears Purifying the Seeping Blood
         And, Purging Your Pain,
         We'd Mend the Past
         With Unconditional Love
           And Forgiveness-
         You'd Be Free At last!

Heavenly Light

         O Heavenly Light
         I Invite You Into
            the Daily Struggles
         The Peaceful Moments
         The Delightful
            Friendships
         And the Difficult Ones
         The Grace
            of the Love Received
         the Ease
            of the Love Given
         The Trust to Continue
            On
         Without Knowing
         the Outcome.

UNCONDITIONAL LOVE

HEART & SOUL

Divine Kiss

Silence Anticipates Your Presence
As you Capture Me
  Unexpectedly
Your first Winter Snowflakes
  Smooching My Face
Like First Love's Unabashed
  Romance
You Lift Me Up to the
  Listening Clouds
Holding Me In the Trees' Embrace.

The Birds' Serenade
  Propels Me Upward
And the Moon Winks at Midnight
  Sending Shivers through the Air
Reminding me of Our
  Transience
In the Wonder of the Universe.

As I Begin My Inevitable
  Departure
My Snow-Sculpted
  Footprints
Bespeak My Heart's Longing
  For More
And the Memory
  Of the Bliss
Of this Divine Kiss
Becomes My Healing Salve
  In Daily Life.

Finding My Love

In My Dreams
I Still Long for First Love's Passion
The Purity of the Kiss
Through the Screen Door at Night.

And I Still Feel the Sting
Of First Love's Rejection
Like a Snake Recoiling
My Skin Thickened
And Love Lost Its Truth.

My College Boyfriend
Brought Back My Laughter
Pulled Back Society's Veil
Exposing the Illusions
As We Marched through
The Protest Years.

And the Drugs Pulled Us Apart.
And the Betrayals Destroyed Us.

My Next Love
Saved Me from Destruction.
A Soulmate for Some Time
Not Meant for All Time
It was Meant to Be
And I Learned My Own Womanness.

Now My Life Partner Is the One
Embracing Me at the Doorstep
Of My Last Earthly Years.
Walking Alongside, Together,
Throughout the Dark Days
And the Light Days.
It is His Arms I Choose to Run Into
For the Rest of My Life.

Reunion 2017

A Kaleidoscope
Merging Past and Present
Our three-generation Chicago Convergence
Creating Luminescent Colors
Of Synchronistic Vibrations.

Poolside on Lake Michigan
Sounds of Laughter and Love
Bring Us Together
Under Common Heritage.

One Twist
Into Reverberations of Yesteryear
When we "Oldsters" were the "Youngsters"
Immersed in Cherished Games.

And - Isn't that our Grandparents
Smiling from Above?

Like Our Jigsaw Puzzle Pursuit
We Meld Together Naturally
Into this Picture
Of Immortality.

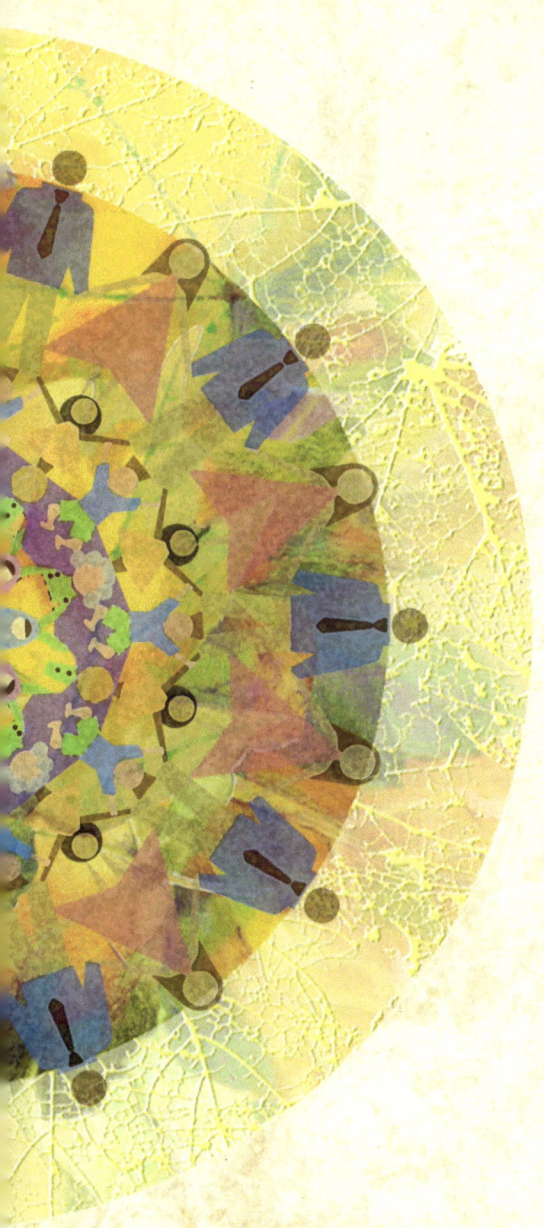

Autumn Sun

Autumn Sun
Beckons Me Onto
Our Sunny Back Deck
This September afternoon.

Trees Reaching Out to Touch
A Deep Familiar Urging
Resurfacing.

My Heart Remembering
My Mom's Last Years
When I asked
"What did you do today?"
Her Peace when she said:
"I Basked in the Warmth
Of the Fall Sunlight."

It is this Longing
Inside MySelf
For her constant Reminders
To "Slow Down"
That still Pulls Me
This Day
For "Time-out"
In the Silence
Of the Breezes

And Pushes Me Many Days
To Stand Apart
From the Rushing Crowd.

How Grateful I Am
For This Soul's Lesson
On this Fall Day.

My Legacy

Over the Horizon
The Water is the Answer-
Soft, Flowing, Rhythmic

Laughing, Playing, Musing
By the Water
I Fall onto the Beach.

Lying in the Sand
My Body-Print
Is my Legacy-
An Outline
Etched in Nature
Immersed in Solace
Next to the Water-
A place for Others
To Lie
In Reflection
Rejuvenation
Remembering.

The Chasm

Torn-Away
Ripped-Away
    From Us
Your Absence
Creating a Chasm
In Our Lives

A Heart-Break
Manifesting
As Empty Spaces/Places
Throughout Our Home

If We Ignore this Crack
We Can Fall Into It
Lost in Oblivion
Of Unspoken Pain

If We Jump Over It
We Will Be Jumping
Ad infinitum
And Drop from Exhaustion

Bridge-Building is Our Choice
Constructed with Memories
Of Joy and Sorrow
Our Gaze Safely Allowing,
Gently Transforming,
Into Our Heart's Remembrance.

Life & Death

Though Life is But a Day and Night
This Time is Mine and Mine the Right
To Gently Love and Painfully Cry
And Never bear a Human Lie.
My Heart in My Hands
And thoughts so Free
These are the Things consisting of Me.
And When I am exhausted,
Worn-out and fulfilled
I'll throw myself in the grass so deep
And there I shall lie,
Content in Sleep.

Death's Birthing

If it Were My Time
I Would Go at Dawn
With Gladness in My Heart

First-
I Would Swim
Deeply in the Sun-Sparkling Lake
Merging with
The Morning Fragrances and Fish
Then, I Would Skim the Water's Surfaces
Reaching from the Shores
to the Islands
to the Marshes
The Sun's Warmth
Upon My Face.

I Would Dance Across the Water
Demystifying the Morning Mist.
Glorifying the Day
With the Purest of Songs.
I Would Stretch
With the Adirondack Evergreens
Finally Reaching Their Pinnacles
And Listening, Knowing
The Sympathy of the Birds.

Next, I Would Fly
To the Top of the Mountain
With One Deep Breath
I Would Soar to Its Peak
And, Lying Naked
Across the Trees
The Mountains
The Oceans
The Universe

Yes,
I Would Say
Yes,
Yes.
Amen

39

Dawn
(Darkness Meets Light)

At Dawn
Where Starlight Meets Sunlight
When Coyotes Dance with the Stars
And Humans Face Spirit
Where the Unseen is Seen
And The Unknown Becomes
Known.

The Light Creeping
Through the Darkness
Revealing Life's Mystery
Compelling Us to Create

At Dawn
When Hearts Beat Strongest
And Lovers Merge Longest

When the Lightness of Day
Meets the Darkness of Night
Creating an Energetic Vortex
Surging with the Promise
Of Possibility.

It Takes the Darkness
To Make the Dawn
The Darkness Pronounces
The Dawn
Announces the Day.

Re-Creation

Lost on the Journey of Life
With Questions Insurmountable
The Ground Like Quicksand
    Beneath Our Feet
Breathlessly We Try to Move Forward
    But Where?

The Media Blinds Us
    To Our Truth
Sinking Us Deeper
    Into Unreality.

When the Third Eye Opens
The Co-Creation Begins.
The Heart Lights the Torch
And Our Own Path Unfolds.

The Knowing Begins
Our Visions Emerging
The Power of Our Words
Merging with the Strength
Of Our Thoughts.

As the Light from Above
Mingles With the Light
From Within
Creating a Brilliance
Revealing
A Universal Vision
Of Unconditional Love.

Destiny's Revelations

A Streak of Lightening Searing
through My Soul
After years of Thunder's Rumblings Forewarnings
Tearing in My Heart
Exposing the Lifelong Gory Guts
Of Truths Withheld.

My Life's Casting Society's Promise Aside
For the Impending Storm
Whose Seawall
Cannot Be Contained.

At Last Releasing the Poisons of Multi-generational
Secrets
Miraculously Evaporating into Life-Giving Air.

As I Witness their Transformation
Into Truths Morphed into Messages
Demanding Revelation
As the Sole Path
To Wound's Healing.

Into the Light
Where Misgivings
Become Forgivings.
And these Scars
Become Our Strength.

Believe

Do you Believe that a Tree's Embrace Heals A Broken Heart?
That the Ocean's Breeze Clears the Mind of Woes?
That the Rain Purifies the Soul?
That the Majestic Mountains take Us to Heaven?
That the Stars - Connection Unites Us All?
And the Moon Lights - Up the World?

You Are A Child of the Universe
Your Blood the Ocean's Waves
Your Life the Soil of the Earth
Your Soul the Star's Constellations

Hug a Tree
Jump into the Ocean
Run in the Rain
Wail at the Moon
And Smile in the Sunlight

It is Your Gift of Life.

By Invitation

Take Me Up to the Ephesian Fields
Effervescent with Starlight
So Bright with White Light
And Blue Skies
Where the Indian's Headdress
Greets Me
With Knowing Eyes
As he Stirs Life's Elixir
With Mortar and Stone.

Breathe Deeply of the Ambiance
Taste Completely this Healing Offering
Each Inhalation Spreads
This Earthly Solace.

His multicolored headdress
Enunciates his Eye's Message:
"Go Forth"

A New Constellation

Two Precious Stars
Forming An Apex
And We-Cosmic Entities,
By Invitation
All together
Creating
A New Constellation.

As if by Divine Design
The Parental Chalice
Is Passed-On.

Celebrating
The Mergence of Two Souls,
the Emergence of
A Greater Consciousness
And the Magnificence
Of A Brighter Galaxy.

On the Verge

I Stared at the Painting
   On the Wall-
Its Archaic Images
In the Antiquated Frame
   Expanding Exponentially
      With my Gaze---
Now the Paint is Breaking Away
   Before my Eyes...
The scroll-like peelings
   Falling onto the floor...
There is no Choice...
   I Must go On...

Reaching-out
   My Nails Tearing
    At the Peeling Paints
Like an Animal
Exposing Its Prey...
Old Wounds Reverberating.

The Emerging Stench A Forewarning...

The First Image fell-out
   Onto the Floor
Catapulting my Body
   Into the Corner:

As I watched,
The Child awoke suddenly...
A Beam of Light streaming into her Face...
Revealing a Crack in the
Old Stone Wall...
The Foreign Light nearly painful to her Eyes...
   Darkness had become her Companion...
How long had she been Underground?
A Pain shot through her rib cage
Her head ached bitterly...
Where was she?
She fought to retrieve memories
Through her Pounding Heart.
Now--the Paint was falling-away Rapidly...
The shreddings heaping onto the floor...
The Images Unfolding.

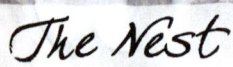

The Nest

She sat Huddled, Cuddled-Up
In the Nest of Nature.
A Pine-Needle Hideout---
In the Midst of Bushes
   Along the Farmyard Driveway...
Her Body Softened, Relaxed...
Here She Was Safe.

Burying Deeply
   Into Leaves, Twigs, Ground...
Nurtured by Earth...
Her Burrowing Beseeching
Mother Earth to Heal
   Her Gaping Wounds
   With Love...
Wounds Not of Reason
But of Spirit...
Asking to Be Revealed...
Begging to Be Healed.

A Friend's Listening Words...
At Last, The Ugliness Exposed
"It was not your fault."

Putridness pervasively
Filling the Room.
It's Revoltedness
Pushing-me-on
To Keep Watching.

Suddenly
Ear-Piercing
Terror Shrieks
Erupting
From the Painting...
My Body pressed against the wall
My Hand-Mitts
Covering my ears...

Screams Now Emitting
Audible Words
Reverberating Within the Cave...
"Let Me Outta Here"
Her Huge Mouth Yelling
So wide
Her Tonsils Visible...
Her Image transformed
Into a Wild Beast...
Banging on the Cave-Rocks
Her Rage-filled Body
Thrown against the Cave...
Creating a Rock-Slide

Struggling to Get Out
Her Biceps Bulging...
She Pulls herself Over the Edge...

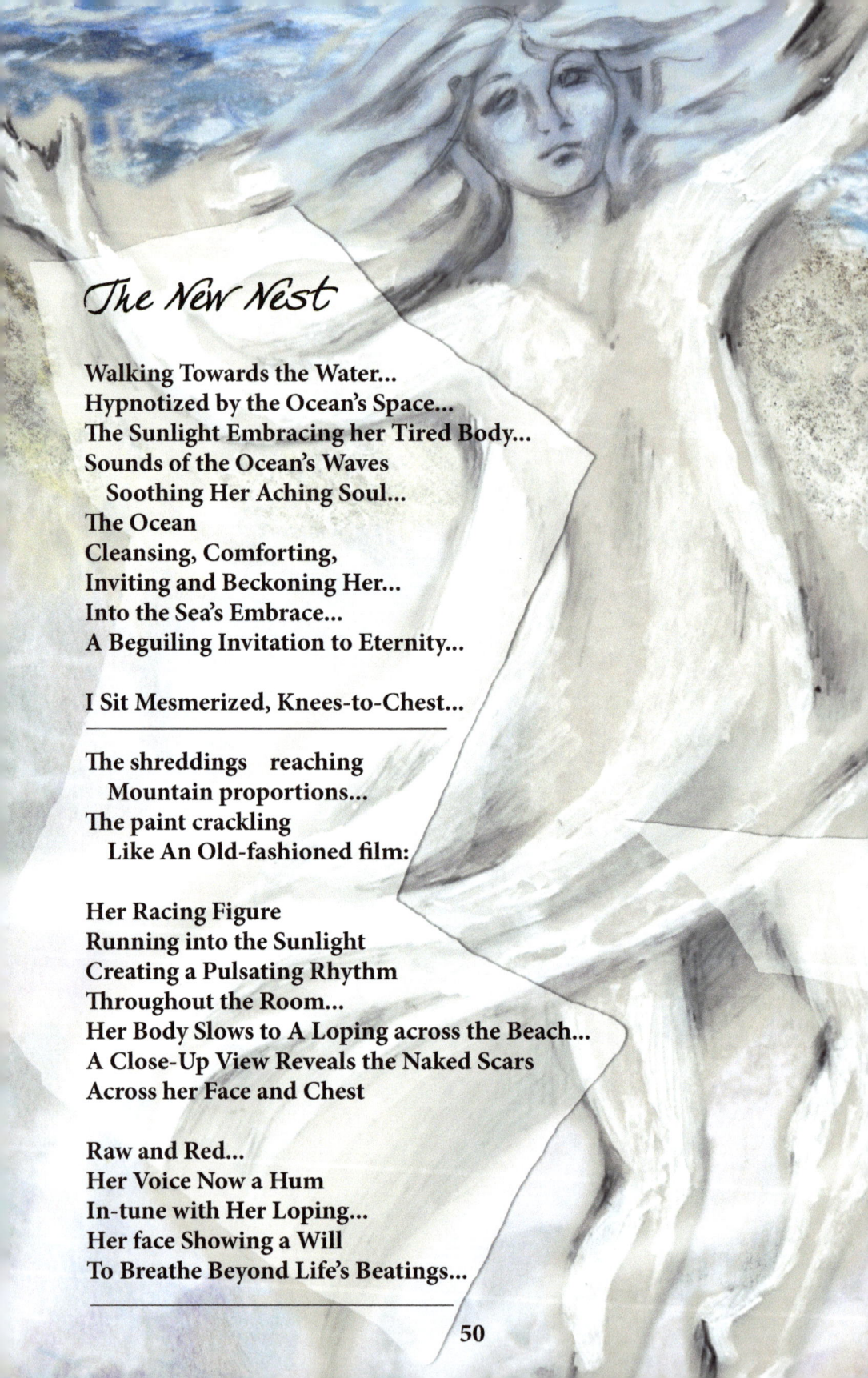

The New Nest

Walking Towards the Water...
Hypnotized by the Ocean's Space...
The Sunlight Embracing her Tired Body...
Sounds of the Ocean's Waves
    Soothing Her Aching Soul...
The Ocean
Cleansing, Comforting,
Inviting and Beckoning Her...
Into the Sea's Embrace...
A Beguiling Invitation to Eternity...

I Sit Mesmerized, Knees-to-Chest...

The shreddings   reaching
    Mountain proportions...
The paint crackling
    Like An Old-fashioned film:

Her Racing Figure
Running into the Sunlight
Creating a Pulsating Rhythm
Throughout the Room...
Her Body Slows to A Loping across the Beach...
A Close-Up View Reveals the Naked Scars
Across her Face and Chest

Raw and Red...
Her Voice Now a Hum
In-tune with Her Loping...
Her face Showing a Will
To Breathe Beyond Life's Beatings...

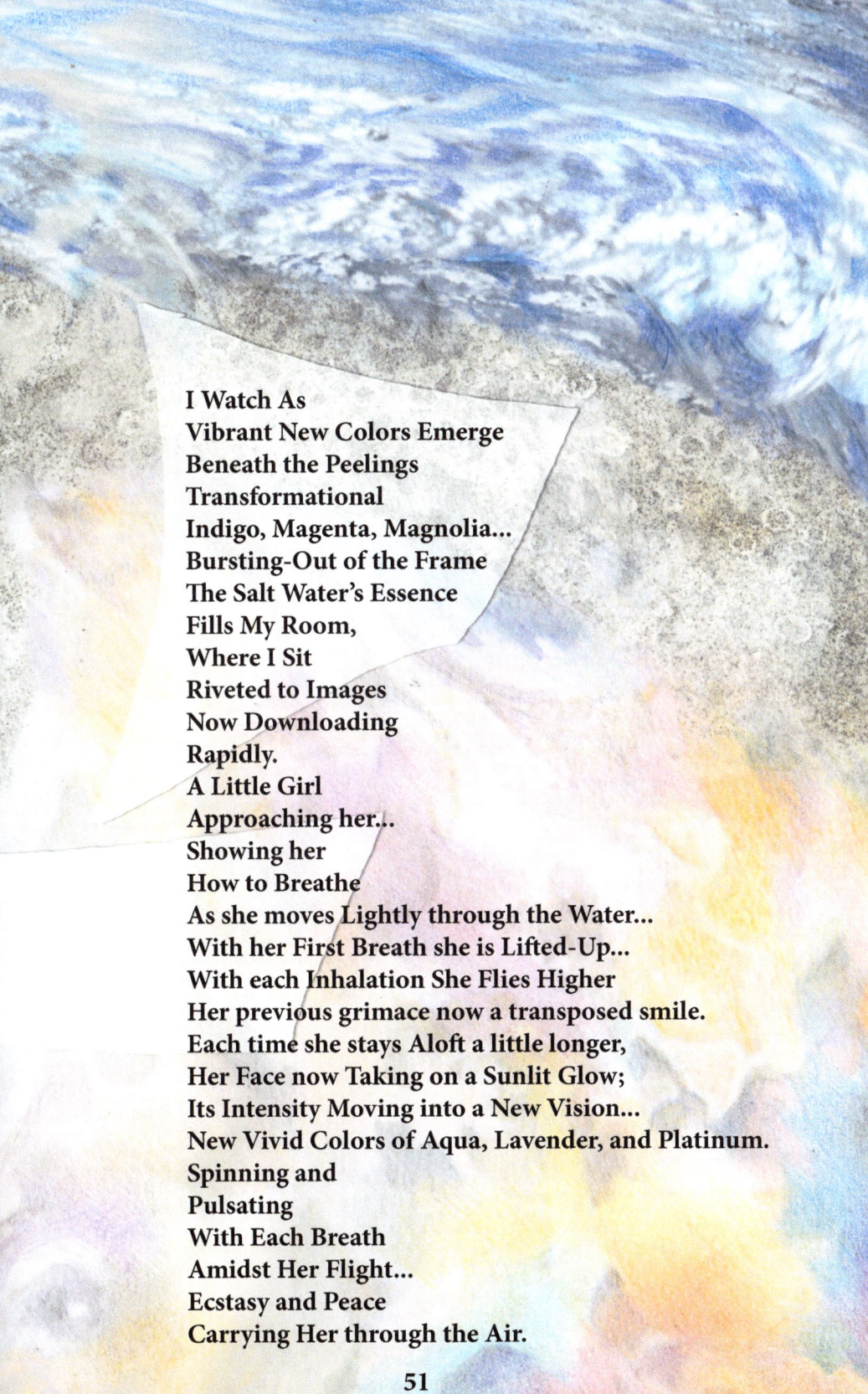

I Watch As
Vibrant New Colors Emerge
Beneath the Peelings
Transformational
Indigo, Magenta, Magnolia...
Bursting-Out of the Frame
The Salt Water's Essence
Fills My Room,
Where I Sit
Riveted to Images
Now Downloading
Rapidly.
A Little Girl
Approaching her...
Showing her
How to Breathe
As she moves Lightly through the Water...
With her First Breath she is Lifted-Up...
With each Inhalation She Flies Higher
Her previous grimace now a transposed smile.
Each time she stays Aloft a little longer,
Her Face now Taking on a Sunlit Glow;
Its Intensity Moving into a New Vision...
New Vivid Colors of Aqua, Lavender, and Platinum.
Spinning and
Pulsating
With Each Breath
Amidst Her Flight...
Ecstasy and Peace
Carrying Her through the Air.

My Jaw Drops
As Her Countenance
Begins to Merge with the Little Girl...
A Wind gusts through the Room...
The Peelings Suck-Up and Evaporating...
I am now Gripping the Picture
So not to be Swept Away...
The Picture Now
Radiating
Its Own
Ambiance.
The Girl-Woman
Flies Higher, Higher,
Lighter, Lighter...
The Smell of Salt-Water
So Strong
I Can Taste it Myself.
I Can See Her Heart's Longing
Feel her Soul's Essence,
I am Clinging to the Frame.

The Next Morning
They Found Me...
Floating on the Water's
Edge...
My Wings Still
Intact...
As They Approached
I Flew
    Away.

The End

Cuando El Luz Entra

Cuando El Luz Entra

El Corazon

La Noche Se Va.

When the Light

Enters

The Heart

The Night

Leaves.

Karen S. Marshall is an illustrator, graphic artist, and textile designer.

Karen likes to draw an atmosphere of fantasy, mystery, and illusion. Her colored pencil drawings bring mythical and heavenly creatures to life in the pages of Edith Lamprecht's thought-provoking mystical verse in "Confluence".

Karen lives with her husband Dan, and her kitty Willow, in Norwich, Connecticut. She enjoys being oceanside at every opportunity, and when she is not drawing or painting, Karen enjoys practicing yoga, Reiki, and photography.

Edith H. Lamprecht loves life in all of its aspects, and enjoys experiencing it in swimming, hiking, meditating, reading, writing, and spending time with her family and friends. Edith lives in Uncasville, Connecticut with her family.

In this book, "Confluence", she shares her Life Journey in her Soulful free verse.

Release the Past
Embrace the Present,
Carry the Light Forward
With Love, Peace,
And Joy.

www.ingramcontent.com/pod-product-compliance
Lightning Source LLC
Chambersburg PA
CBHW040743250626
47164CB00006BA/163